SandCastle

Around the World

Cultures
Around the World

Kelly Doudna

Consulting Editor, Diane Craig, M.A./Reading Specialist

ABDO Publishing Company

Published by ABDO Publishing Company, 4940 Viking Drive, Edina, Minnesota 55435.

Printed in the United States.

Credits
Edited by: Pam Price
Curriculum Coordinator: Nancy Tuminelly
Cover and Interior Design and Production: Mighty Media
Photo Credits: BananaStock Ltd., Corbis Images, Stockbyte

Library of Congress Cataloging-in-Publication Data

Doudna, Kelly, 1963-
    Cultures around the world / Kelly Doudna.
        p. cm. -- (Around the world)
    Includes index.
    Summary: Describes the many cultures found around the world.
    ISBN 1-59197-566-2
        1. Culture--juvenile literature. [1. Culture. 2. Manners and customs.] I. Title.

TEM

fessional team of educators, reading specialists, and content developers around five essential components that include phonemic awareness, phonics, vocabulary, text comprehension, and fluency. All books are written, reviewed, and leveled for guided reading, early intervention reading, and Accelerated Reader® programs and designed for use in shared, guided, and independent reading and writing activities to support a balanced approach to literacy instruction.

Let Us Know

After reading the book, SandCastle would like you to tell us your stories about reading. What is your favorite page? Was there something hard that you needed help with? Share the ups and downs of learning to read. We want to hear from you! To get posted on the ABDO Publishing Company Web site, send us e-mail at:

sandcastle@abdopub.com

SandCastle Level: Fluent

People around the world have different cultures.

Understanding
and accepting
these differences is
important.

It makes the world a more peaceful place to live.

Paco and his mother speak Spanish.

They live in Argentina.

Marie buys bread at the neighborhood bakery.

She lives in France.

Chen takes part in a New Year's celebration.

He lives in China.

In China the New Year starts on a different day each year.

Del and his friends
like to play rugby.

They live in Australia.

Erik wears lederhosen.

He lives in Germany.

Sue and Lori like country music.

They live in the United States.

What customs in your culture are different from other cultures around the world?

Did You Know?

Spanish is the fourth most spoken language in the world, behind Mandarin, English, and Hindi.

It is widely believed that the sport of rugby started when a soccer player picked up the ball and ran with it.

There are more than 35,000 bakeries in France.

The Chinese New Year begins with the new moon that occurs between January 21 and February 19.

Glossary

accept. to think of as normal, right, or unavoidable

bakery. a place where breads and pastries are made

celebration. a party or festival held to mark a special occasion

custom. a tradition practiced by people in a particular region or area

different. not alike

lederhosen. leather shorts with suspenders that are traditionally worn in Europe in the Alps

peaceful. calm, free from disagreement

rugby. a game similar to football

About SandCastle™

A professional team of educators, reading specialists, and content developers created the SandCastle™ series to support young readers as they develop reading skills and strategies and increase their general knowledge. The SandCastle™ series has four levels that correspond to early literacy development in young children. The levels are provided to help teachers and parents select the appropriate books for young readers.

Emerging Readers
(no flags)

Beginning Readers
(1 flag)

Transitional Readers
(2 flags)

Fluent Readers
(3 flags)

These levels are meant only as a guide. All levels are subject to change.

To see a complete list of SandCastle™ books and other nonfiction titles from ABDO Publishing Company, visit **www.abdopub.com** or contact us at:

4940 Viking Drive, Edina, Minnesota 55435 • 1-800-800-1312 • fax: 1-952-831-1632